SPECULATIVE FICTION

OH, THAT'S GOOD, TOO!

52 MORE WRITING PROMPTS YOU NEVER KNEW YOU NEEDED. BUT SERIOUSLY... YOU DO.

R.A. CLARKE

COPYRIGHT

Copyright © 2022 Rachael Clarke

Print ISBN: 978-1-7771219-6-9
Epub ISBN: 978-1-7771219-7-6

All rights reserved. No part of this publication may be reproduced, stored in a retrieval system, or transmitted in any form or by any means, electronic, mechanical, recording or otherwise, without the prior written permission of the publisher. For permissions, please contact via: www.pageturnpress.com.

Published by Page Turn Press, Portage la Prairie, Manitoba.
Cover Design by Rachael Clarke (PTP Design).
Edited by Charlie Knight.

Available in eBook and Paperback.

The characters and events mentioned in this book are fictitious and the work of the author's imagination. Any similarity to real persons, living or dead, events or localities is coincidental and not intended by the author.

Page Turn Press
2022

To my high school English teacher, Ms. Paulette Buizer. Thanks for supporting my writing and encouraging my dream to publish a book someday.

I owe you a coffee.

INTRODUCTION

Greetings, and welcome to my humble book. I see you are a speculative fiction writer. How do I know that? Well, even if you hadn't just purchased this compilation of writing prompts—which you did—I'd still know. Your creativity is written all over your expression, implied in the tilt of your posture (earned from hours of vigorous typing), and complimented by a fantastical twinkle in your eye.

Do you not believe I see it? Hmm...well, perhaps you've caught me in a playful fib. Or consider the inexplicable possibility I truly can! Push your mind into the speculative realm and look around you. Could I be a forest faery hiding in your lampshade? A ghost who won't leave you alone? Maybe I've opened a fissure in time, and I'm now hiding in the closet just to mess with your head.

Okay, okay...yes, you caught me in a fib. I certainly wish I had power to slice fissures through time, among other extraordinary things, but sadly, I cannot. Nobody can—yet.

Except there is one way we can: by writing speculative fiction. It allows us to create and experience whatever reality we dare to dream up. If I want to charge into battle against an army of Orcs to save my struggling kingdom, hand me my sword. Or maybe I want to sneak a ride in a star cruiser to a new planet and fall madly in love with an alien named Zed. Heck yeah! That kind of versatility is the joy of speculative fiction, and I'm excited to dive into that with you.

Within this book, you'll find 52 ideas that popped out of my uniquely twisted grey matter. I've meticulously brainstormed each one to fuel your writing flame, covering topics from dark to light, cityscapes to spaceships, cryptids to fairytale creatures, robots to faeries, and everything in between.

You can choose to take it slowly and work your way through the book, earmark whatever pages inspire you most, or if you're feeling adventurous, take my 52-Week Challenge: write a shiny new story with a fresh prompt each week over the course of a year. That's some off-the-charts intensity, right there! Consider yourself dared.

And if you DO *complete* the challenge, make sure you write to me and brag. Not a humble brag, either. I want to see an excessive peppering of exclamation marks and a liberal use of all caps. I'll even send you a digital badge to flaunt.

Lastly, whatever you do with this book (and please don't say it'll make nice toilet paper. Well, unless you've somehow time-warped back into 2020 and the grocery store shelves are bare. I suppose that's forgivable), make sure to have a blast! Brew a cup of joe, curl up in your coziest nook, and write—write hard. Breathe life into these prompts like the talented word-wizards you are.

I believe all writers—regardless of age or skill level—are true magicians. Why? Because with the nimble flick of a sharpened lead-core wand, *anything* is possible.

So, are you ready to dive in and make some magic happen? Good. I believe in you.

R.A. Clarke

Be yourself; everyone else is already taken...

◆*Oscar Wilde*◆

SHALL WE GET STARTED?

1

Oh, the stories you could tell...

As a professional window washer, you're fairly confident you've seen it all. But nothing prepares you for what you glimpse in suite 120C.

2

You're perched on the edge of a bridge, contemplating the horrible hand you've been dealt in life, when you see a strange shimmering reflection move in the water below. You lean forward to see it more clearly, and your fingers slip.

3

So, skydiving... It seemed like such a great choice for a first date. Until you landed on something completely invisible in the middle of the air.

4

You go to the fair and get sick riding the teacups. Thankfully, you make it off in time to empty your stomach contents *behind* the ride rather than on it. When you glance up, a tiny pair of eyes peer back at you from beneath the ride's shadowy platform. You've never seen any creature quite like it, and it looks trapped.

Aw…you can't just leave it there.

5

Milkshakes are all the rage these days—they've got flavours for everything. Emotion shakes help people regulate. Drug shakes get people high, keep them awake to study, or induce much-needed sleep. However, a new flavour has been making the rounds, and it's having unexpected side effects.

6

You've always been very careful to hide the gills in your wrists. You wear long sleeves, gloves, wide watches, and decorative wrist bands you designed yourself. But while out for a jog one night, you get kidnapped, and your captors expose your wrists. You fear the worst, until they surprise you with a one-of-a-kind job offer you can't refuse.

7

The world's first weather modification system is officially put into action, but nobody could've predicted what would happen. The outcome is extreme. Impossible fog, flooding, freezing, scorching...but the act of surviving shifts into a new gear when a storm rolls in that infuses an electrical charge into everything conductive.

8

Your partner in crime is an advanced A.I. you call Benny. It's strong, fast, reliable, and has saved your sorry behind too many times to count. But when Benny slips a gear in your latest heist and you barely make it out alive, you discover an alluring rogue service bot is to blame.

Is it even possible for robots to feel attraction? To find love? Should you set them up on a date?

9

A sinkhole opens up on the outskirts of the city, swallowing a large chunk of highway and several vehicles. Your main character is on the search and rescue team, and discovers dozens of connecting tunnels, golden wall plates covered with unknown hieroglyphs, and other signs of ancient civilization in the gaping cavern unearthed.

10

Your sneakers inexplicably come to life, which is incredible…until it's not. They're impossible to deal with. They never shut up, and can't agree on anything. You've tried unsuccessfully to take them off. Plus, between you and me, lefty is a real jerk.

THIS SEEMS LIKE A GREAT SPOT FOR A MOTIVATIONAL QUOTE, DON'T YA THINK?

HERE YOU GO!

"For success, attitude is equally important as ability..."

◆*Walter Scott*◆

We are our own worst critics, right? Try to remember there's enough rejection in the writing world without adding your own negativity to the pile. If the glass stays half-full, so too might the opportunities.

11

Your kid is sensitive to noise—gets over stimulated easily—so, being the good parent you are, you buy noise cancellation headphones. They're nice ones, with a feature to play music, too.

When your child starts saying and doing incredibly kind and loving things, you're baffled. It remains a mystery until you happen to put on the headphones by chance one day and hear a God-like voice speak.

12

Ah! It's spring and love is in the air.

No, literally—pheromones are flying all over the place, causing unexpected chaos as a bizarre coral-coloured fog permeates the city.

13

Your beloved grandfather recently passed away, leaving you an extensive and rather outdated hat collection that, when stimulated, proves to be anything but dull.

14

As the wind swirls and pushes,

I lift up off the ground.

Oh, how the sky calls to me!

I this home I have found?

15

A mysterious set of stairs has appeared in a field behind your farmhouse. They lead to the surface from…somewhere underground. They're smooth metal and don't have a spec of dirt on them. What's even more mystifying is the fresh set of tracks leading away from them.

16

You lose your lucky belt buckle, and the entire galaxy feels like it might implode. That's probably because it literally will if you don't get it back asap. Someone must've figured out the secret you're protecting and stole it! Ugh, what a mess. Guess that belt wasn't so lucky after all.

17

Your skin tingles whenever you walk by the new painting in the hallway. It feels like someone's watching you—which is ridiculous, because its not even a portrait. It's a retro diner surrounded by towering buildings. Then a glimmer of movement draws your eye. The light turns on in the diner. A figure stares at you from one of the windows.

18

You board a transit bus rigged with a bomb that will explode if the speed falls below 50mph...

Just kidding! Here's the real prompt:

Your shadow develops sentience and can compel your feet to do whatever it wishes. Unlucky for you, it's a thrill seeker.

19

You find an ancient looking letter inside a bottle that washed ashore, but this is no love letter...

20

At the top of a freshly built skyscraper, two construction workers set aside their long-time rivalry to build something amazing of their own. However, when someone sneaks onto the site and taints their design, the pair inadvertently create a glaring beacon for demons instead.

21

You put on your new reading glasses for the first time, and they show you things. Messed up things that make no sense yet seem vividly real. Naturally, you freak out and try to take the spectacles off, but they won't budge. The images continue—merciless barrages that make you question reality itself.

READY FOR ANOTHER INSPIRATIONAL QUOTE?

HERE'S A BEAUT.

"Give me six hours to chop down a tree and I will spend the first four sharpening the axe..."

✦Abraham Lincoln✦

To learn about and hone one's craft is so important. Why not be prepared instead of making unnecessary mistakes? For writers, that can mean taking courses, watching webinars, reading books in your preferred genres, and/or beta reading for other authors.

22

Nobody knew just what you could do;

You kept your skills carefully pulled into place.

But safe in your home completely alone,

You revel in morphing your entire face.

23

A quaint and very isolated mountain town receives an otherworldly and unexpectedly smelly visitor right before a huge snowstorm hits and closes down all the roads.

24

A middle-aged woman who never had children finds an infant left in a metal wash tub on her doorstep. The baby is covered in mud! Horrified, she takes the child inside and pours a bath. However, she soon realizes the child is inexplicably unique, and the mud makes a lot more sense now.

25

After a bizarre incident involving a shock from an electrical outlet, your main character realizes his umbrella has taken on a life of its own, bestowing insight and agility whenever it's used.

26

Two incognito wizards meet and sparks fly at the big "noodle off" event during Pastafield's 78th annual Mac n' Cheese Festival.

27

When a jaded food reviewer hiding a dangerous secret walks into a bakery, he meets the woman of his dreams while simultaneously tasting the worst pretzel of his life. How has this bakery stayed afloat selling product like that? After the tingles start, it won't be long before he learns the answer.

28

A stock car race heats up when the rival pit crew sabotages your main character's car, crossing a major line that can't be ignored. How far will both drivers go to win? And what happens when they find out the race was never real to begin with?

29

Competitive fishing takes dangerous spin and skyrockets into the limelight when a legit sighting of a Jurassic fish the size of a killer whale is confirmed during a televised event.

30

You and your fiancé rented a house for a weeklong getaway and find an old leather journal inside a hidden crevice between bricks in the old hearth. You've never seen the book before, yet it's about you. Fresh words appear and then change on the pages as you flip. And when your fiancé reads it, it's about him.

NEED ANOTHER SERVING OF MOTIVATION?

DEVOUR THIS ONE.

"Well done is better than well said…"
◆Benjamin Franklin◆

It's easy to talk about writing. I liken dreaming up new ideas to dating in a way. It's fresh, fun, and exciting at first. But, just like relationships, that doesn't last forever. Eventually, writers must get the thoughts out of their heads and onto the page.

31

Breaking news: a new hybrid species of robin has migrated into our territory. Reports coming in confirm they are hyper-aggressive and territorial, with a poisonous beak. Don't let them peck at you!

32

Eligible Knights compete to win the favour of a noble woman. Her charmed love is said to bestow a wealth of fortune and opportunity upon the lucky receiver. But the noble woman does not appreciate being looked upon as a prize, and winning her affection proves far more challenging than anyone imagined. That's when a new and unprecedented competition is announced. One that sends ripples throughout the entire kingdom.

33

"The boat's sinking! Ready the lifeboats!"

"This is all your fault! If you hadn't taken this job, we wouldn't be in this mess."

"Don't you dare go blamin' me. It was your cursed trinket that projected our map in the first place—"

"Shh! Captain, look behind you."

"Don't try to distract—"

"Quiet! Just look out the window. *Now*."

"For the love of... What in the briny sea is that?"

34

Something is making snow sculptures come alive and cause all kinds of chaos in a cozy mountain town. Things get even weirder after an abominable snowman sighting, and then a bizarrely dressed figure sporting silver icicles for hair shows up claiming to be Jack Frost himself.

35

An alien aboard a deep space exploration ship learns from a human crewmate what Christmas is all about, then decides to showcase what a holiday looks like on his planet. It shocks everyone.

36

An explosives specialist in a new off-world colony has no clue she's getting called to diffuse bombs she herself has set.

37

A person with Chromophobia (fear of colors) never leaves home without their custom colour dampening goggles. However, when a sudden life or death situation forces them to face their fear, will they wind up a survivor or a victim of calamity?

38

A person develops the telepathic power to call upon any superhero, and that hero would be compelled beyond their will to comply. When word gets out, your main character simultaneously becomes the most famous and loathed person in town.

39

A freak fire tornado sears through a farming community and unleashes waves of acidic rain as it pins a struggling family inside the wreckage of their rural home. All but one of them is injured, and with no medical supplies on hand to keep infection at bay, they're fighting the clock to hold out until rescue comes. *If* rescue can come at all.

40

The house your main character inherited was built in the early 1900's. Renovations are long over due. But when the contractor rips up all the rotten wood treads to fix the staircase, he finds a unique metal time capsule hidden within each step. What is found preserved inside is unfathomable.

QUOTE BREAK!

LET THIS NUGGET OF WISDOM SINK IN...

"Patience is bitter,
but its fruit is sweet..."
◆Aristotle◆

Writing takes time. It's so easy to become impatient, to crave that moment when you finally reach the end of a story and get that glorious thrill of success and satisfaction. That's the sweet fruit.

41

The rebellious teenage daughter of a recently separated faery couple runs away from home in a huff, promptly stumbling into a troll garden and landing herself in serious danger. Desperate, the couple works together and buries their troubles in order to attempt a daring rescue mission. But everyone knows troubles never stay buried.

42

Remember that time you seduced me, implanted me with your oozing parasite which sucked half the blood from my body, and then ended up turning me into your helpless minion?

Ah, yes. Good times...

43

Your steam train is on a tight deadline, and you're running low on coal. As you slow down, a group of horseback-riding robbers catch up to you, and in no time, you've been taken hostage.

After they tie you up in the corner, you watch helplessly as the leader brandishes a handful of odd-looking rocks and tosses them into the fire. What happens next sends your mind reeling.

44

Living a life in neon means hitting up raging parties and pushing hijacked tech. At least it did, until the wrong kind of tech—rare and dangerous—falls into your hands. What's worse, someone you *really* don't want to meet will surely be looking for it.

45

The laziest boom operator on set accidentally discovers that every single celebrity in Hollywood is actually an advanced life-like AI robot.

46

Bigfoot has been proven authentic! A mated pair was discovered, tranquilized, and placed in a zoo exhibit. But when the first ever Bigfoot baby is born in captivity, it has very little hair. In fact, it looks perfectly human, sparking discord and questions about their origins, sentience, and basic rights.

47

A nature loving teenager stumbles upon a frozen Alaskan wood frog and remembers they don't die if they freeze. He takes it home and sets it under a heat lamp, waiting eagerly to watch it thaw from the inside out like he'd read about. Holy cats, he didn't read anything about an explosive and instantaneous reproduction cycle, though!

48

The soul of every person lost to calamity or misfortune within the subway system gathers on Platform Nine every day, patiently waiting for their "final train" to the afterlife. They stand in their designated spaces, invisible as the oblivious world carries on. Except for Jack. He sees them.

49

"Who—or *what*—are all these pictures of?"

"What? You don't know, the fly man of Marx hill?"

"The *fly man?* No clue. The pics look super fake."

"Well, most are. But come here...look at this one."

"Yeah, the wings look more realistic on that one."

"Right? I'm actually making a documentary—trying to catch it on film. Wanna help?"

50

It's true! Unicorns are real. Their existence has been extensively reported by the lone survivor of an ill-fated exploration trip to a cave nestled within a remote rainforest location. But before you get too excited, it turns out they're not as pretty or majestic as the fairytales say.

51

Wyvern's went extinct ages ago—huge beasts with venomous tails that ravaged the land. But when a team of scientists discover perfectly preserved wyvern DNA in a deep-sea cavern, they waste no time cloning it. Sadly, the experiment goes awry, creating an unexpected pint-sized problem.

52

Priceless treasures, hidden truths, scandalous tales, and a boat load of charmed herbal tea flips the latest meeting of the Maid Marion Sisterhood upside down. Or maybe it's finally right side up!

HERE'S ONE LAST QUOTE FOR THE ROAD.

"It does not matter how slowly you go, as long as you do not stop."

◆*Confucius*◆

Take your time to do your best work. Make it something you'll be proud of, and don't ever give up.

THANKS FOR READING

I hope this book was everything you thought it would be—hopefully more. I created this writing prompt series because I never have as much time to write as I'd like. My mischievous kiddos always keep me on my toes. Yep, when people say there are never enough hours in the day, they ain't lying. But that doesn't stop my brain from drumming up ideas. My thinker never takes a break, even when I'm dying for one (seriously, I need to fix that). So, I finally decided...why not just share the wealth? While I love the ideas that pop into my thought bubbles, I can't possibly write them all. Thus, this book was born!

Now, for those who skim read but haven't started writing yet, remember, you can use any part of these prompts. Blend them, twist them, modify them, break them apart—anything you like. Create a concept that's 100% yours, then write the bajeezus out of it. These prompts are meant to be sparks of inspiration, tiny droplets in a rolling sea waiting to be sailed... and my gifts to you.

Hey, speaking of gifts, if you liked this book, make sure to pick up the first in the series—*Oh, That's Good...* Also, check out my published short fiction at www.rachaelclarkewrites.com by clicking on the R.A. Clarke tab. While there, if you have kids or relatives in the 7 to 10-year-old range, take a peek at my children's chapter book *The Big Ol' Bike*. It's a heartwarming contemporary tale about family, friendship, and finding confidence in the face of bullying.

Whether you enjoyed reading, took the 52-Week Challenge, or simply want to recommend this book to others, I'd appreciate it if you could leave an honest review online. Not only do I love helping writers find new sparks of inspiration, but I also love to hear your valuable thoughts and feedback.

Well, I suppose it's time to stop blabbing and wrap this up. Thanks to everyone who helped this book become a reality and thank you to all the readers out there.

Happy writing! Let the magic flow.

R.A. Clarke

ABOUT THE AUTHOR

R.A. Clarke is a former police officer turned stay-at-home mom from Portage la Prairie, MB. She shares life with a sport-aholic husband, two adorable children, and a faithful canine companion she'd never leave home without. Besides sipping coffee on the deck, R.A. enjoys plotting fantastical novels, multi-genre short fiction, and writes/illustrates children's literature as Rachael Clarke. She has won both The Writer's Games and Writer's Weekly international competitions, and was named a finalist for the 2021 Futurescapes Award. R.A.'s work has been published by Polar Borealis Magazine, Sinister Smile Press, and Cloaked Press LLC, among others.

To follow and read selections of R.A.'s short fiction, check out her website: www.rachaelclarkewrites.com.

Other social media:

Twitter: @raclarkewrites
Instagram: @rachaelclarkewrites
Facebook: https://www.facebook.com/raclarkeauthor
(short fiction and adult novels)
https://www.facebook.com/rachaelclarkewrites
(children's literature)

52 original speculative fiction prompts to inspire and spark your creative flame. Spin, switch, expand, elevate, and transform these concepts into your own. Oh, and don't forget to have fun while you're at it. Are you ready to dive in and write that next great story?

Available wherever books are sold.

www.pageturnpress.com

www.ingramcontent.com/pod-product-compliance
Lightning Source LLC
Chambersburg PA
CBHW030041100526
44590CB00011B/284